Praying Mantises

by Helen Frost

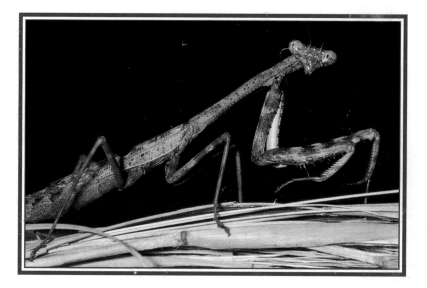

Consulting Editor: Gail Saunders-Smith, Ph.D.

Consultant: Gary A. Dunn, Director of Education, Young Entomologists' Society

Pebble Books

an imprint of Capstone Press
Mankato, Minnesota

Pebble Books are published by Capstone Press
151 Good Counsel Drive, P.O. Box 669, Mankato, Minnesota 56002
http://www.capstone-press.com

Library of Congress Cataloging-in-Publication Data
Frost, Helen, 1949–
    Praying mantises/by Helen Frost.
    p. cm.—(Insects)
    Includes bibliographical references (p. 23) and index.
    ISBN 0-7368-0853-1
    1. Praying mantis—Juvenile literature. [1. Praying mantis.] I. Title. II. Insects
(Mankato, Minn.)
QL508.M4 F76 2001
595.7'27—dc21   00-009676

Summary: Simple text and photographs describe the physical characteristics and
habits of praying mantises.

Note to Parents and Teachers

The Insects series supports national science standards on units
on the diversity and unity of life. The series shows that animals
have features that help them live in different environments. This
book describes praying mantises and illustrates their parts and
habits. The photographs support early readers in understanding
the text. The repetition of words and phrases helps early readers
learn new words. This book also introduces early readers to subject-
specific vocabulary words, which are defined in the Words to Know
section. Early readers may need assistance to read some words and
to use the Table of Contents, Words to Know, Read More, Internet
Sites, and Index/Word List sections of the book.

Table of Contents

4

Praying mantises live
in gardens and fields.

6

Praying mantises use camouflage to hide from predators.

eyes

Praying mantises have two large eyes made of many lenses.

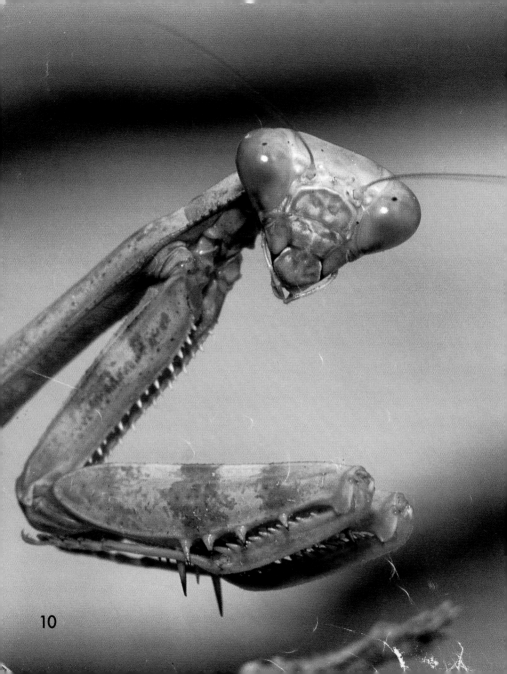

10

Praying mantises can turn their heads in many directions.

wings

Praying mantises
have four wings.

Praying mantises fold
their front legs. They
wait to attack their prey.

Praying mantises quickly reach out to catch their prey.

17

18

Praying mantises use their strong front legs to hold their prey.

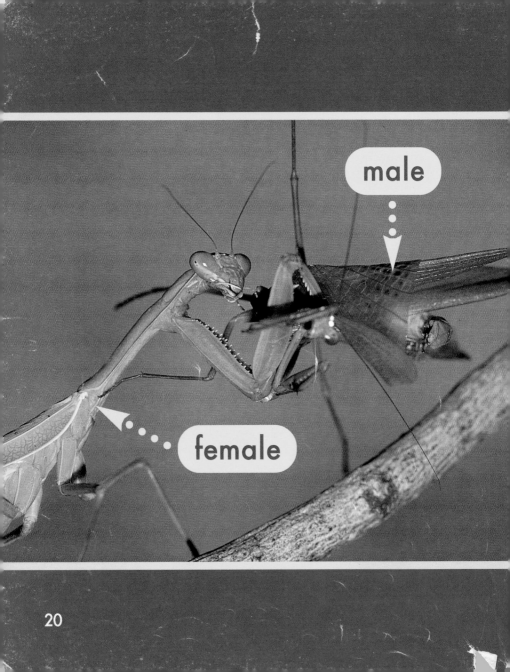

male

female

Some female praying
mantises eat their mates.

Words to Know

camouflage—coloring that makes something look like its surroundings

eye—a body part used for seeing; praying mantises have two large, compound eyes made of many small lenses; their large eyes can sense very small movements; praying mantises also have three small eyes that can sense light.

female—an animal that can give birth to young animals or lay eggs

mate—one partner of a pair of animals

predator—an animal that hunts and eats other animals; bats, birds, and wasps are predators of praying mantises.

prey—an animal that is hunted and eaten; praying mantises usually eat live prey such as bees and grasshoppers.

turn—to spin, rotate, or change direction; praying mantises are the only insects that can turn their heads to look back.

Read More

Berger, Melvin. *Buzz!: A Book about Insects.* Hello Science Reader! New York: Scholastic, 2000.

Brimner, Larry Dane. *Praying Mantises.* A True Book. New York: Children's Press, 1999.

Dussling, Jennifer. *Bugs! Bugs! Bugs!* Eyewitness Readers. New York: D K Publishing, 1998.

Stefoff, Rebecca. *Praying Mantis.* Living Things. New York: Benchmark Books, 1997.

Internet Sites

Praying Mantis
http://www.EnchantedLearning.com/subjects/insects/mantids/Prayingmantidprintout.shtml

Praying Mantis
http://www.insecta-inspecta.com/mantids/praying

Praying Mantis Fact Sheet
http://www.ag.ohio-state.edu/~ohioline/hyg-fact/2000/2154.html

Index/Word List

Word Count: 78
Early-Intervention Level: 10

Editorial Credits

Mari C. Schuh, editor; Timothy Halldin, cover designer; Kia Bielke, production
  designer; Kimberly Danger, photo researcher

Photo Credits

Dwight R. Kuhn, 8, 12, 14
James P. Rowan, 18
Laura Riley/Bruce Coleman Inc., 16
Robert & Linda Mitchell, 20
Visuals Unlimited/Maslowski, cover; Rick Poley, 1; Gary W. Carter, 4;
  Joe McDonald, 6; G and C Merker, 10

24